Exam Success in
Physics
for Cambridge IGCSE®
Practical Workbook

T0346888

Primrose Kitten

OXFORD
UNIVERSITY PRESS

OXFORD
UNIVERSITY PRESS

Great Clarendon Street, Oxford, OX2 6DP, United Kingdom

Oxford University Press is a department of the University of Oxford. It furthers the University's objective of excellence in research, scholarship, and education by publishing worldwide. Oxford is a registered trade mark of Oxford University Press in the UK and in certain other countries

First published in 2022

British Library Cataloguing in Publication Data
Data available

978-1-38-200643-9

3 5 7 9 10 8 6 4 2

Paper used in the production of this book is a natural, recyclable product made from wood grown in sustainable forests. The manufacturing process conforms to the environmental regulations of the country of origin.

Printed and bound by CPI Group (UK) Ltd, Croydon, CR0 4YY

Acknowledgements

®IGCSE is the registered trademark of Cambridge International Examinations.

The publisher and author would like to thank the following for permission to use photographs and other copyright material:

Cover: kdshutterman/Shutterstock Stock Photo. Photos: p10: Devil Keung; and p11: tuu sitt/Shutterstock.

Artwork by Q2A Media Services Pvt. Ltd., Aptara, Jeff Bowles, Roger Courthold, Mike Ogden, Jeff Edwards, Russell Walker, Clive Goodyer, Jamie Sneddon, Tech Graphics, Oxford Designers and Ilustrators Ltd., Tech-Set Ltd., Six Red Marbles, Nelson Thornes Ltd., Peter Banks, IFA Design, Plymouth UK, and OUP.

Every effort has been made to contact copyright holders of material reproduced in this book. Any omissions will be rectified in subsequent printings if notice is given to the publisher.

Links to third party websites are provided by Oxford in good faith and for information only. Oxford disclaims any responsibility for the materials contained in any third party website referenced in this work.

This Practical Workbook refers to the Cambridge IGCSE® Physics (0625) and Cambridge O Level Physics (5054) Syllabuses published by Cambridge Assessment International Education.

This work has been developed independently from and is not endorsed by or otherwise connected with Cambridge Assessment International Education.

Experimental skills and investigations make up 20% of the assessment weighting in Cambridge IGCSE® and are examined in Papers 5 and 6. This book will help students prepare for the practical exams. Students being able to recall the practicals they have studied in class will not be enough to get the marks. They need to be able to adapt that knowledge to new situations; find errors in practicals; and plan and improve practicals. This workbook is designed to fully prepare students for success in these exams.

The exam success practical workbook:

- covers the practical skills needed for Papers 5 and 6

- allows students to develop their experimental skills

- provides a wide range test questions to assess performance in practicals.

Contents

1 Measurement of physical quantities such as length, volume or force

1. A student wants to investigate the relationship between the volume of a ball and the distance that the ball rolls.

   Plan an experiment to investigate this. You should include:

   - a key control variable and an explanation of how it will be controlled

   - any apparatus that will be used

   - a brief explanation of how to carry out the experiment

   - how you will obtain results

   - how you will ensure that the results are reliable

   - a description of the type of graph that could be drawn from the results.

   You may include a diagram to help you to explain your plan.

Exam tip

Tick off each of the bullet points as you refer to them in your answer – that way you won't miss anything out!

....

....

....

....

....

....

....

....

....

....

....

....

.... [6]

2. A student wants to investigate the relationship between the length of an electrical conductor and its resistance. She uses the conductors shown below in an electrical circuit and measures their resistance.

   a. First, she measures the lengths of the conductors. Use the ruler, which is marked in millimetres, to find the length of each of these conductors.

   i.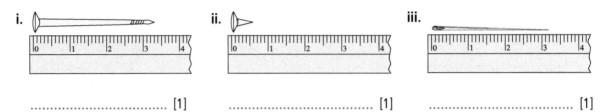

   .... [1]   .... [1]   .... [1]

   b. Explain why a ruler marked in centimetres only would not be suitable to use for this.

   ....

   .... [2]

   c. The student measures the length and resistance of some more conductors (made of the same material and of the same diameter) and plots a graph of the results.

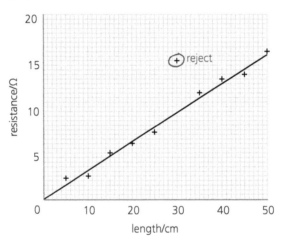

   i. Explain why the point at 29 cm is rejected.

   ....

   .... [2]

   ii. Use the graph to predict the resistance of a 20-cm long conductor.

   .... [2]

   iii. A second student uses the same data points and draws a line of best fit at a shallower angle so that it does not go through the point (0, 0). Explain why this is incorrect.

   Exam tip

   Use construction lines on your graph, to show how you work out your answer.

   ....

   .... [2]

d. Explain whether or not the objects measured in part **a** are suitable for comparing against each other in this experiment.

....

....

.... [3]

3. a. Calculate the volume of this cuboid. Give the unit with your answer.

....

.... [2]

b. A student wants to measure the volume of an irregularly shaped object, such as a stone. They use the equipment shown in the diagram. Explain how they can use this equipment to measure the volume without knowing the depth, length or height of the object.

....

....

....

....

....

....

....

....

....

....

....

....

.... [2]

4. The student rolls a ball along the floor. They use a metre rule to measure how far it travels and how long it takes to come to rest.

   a. The student draws the following table in which to record their results. List **four** improvements that could be made to the table.

mass	length	time

   ....

   ....

   ....

   ....

   ....

   .... [4]

   b. The student then rolls the ball down a slope. They want to measure the distance the ball rolls from where it was released. They use a metre rule and measure the distance shown in the diagram. Explain the error that the student has made.

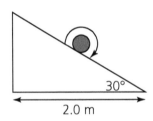

30°

2.0 m

   ....

   ....

   ....

   .... [2]

5. a. Newton meters can be used to determine the force exerted by an object. Write the values shown on each of these newton meters.

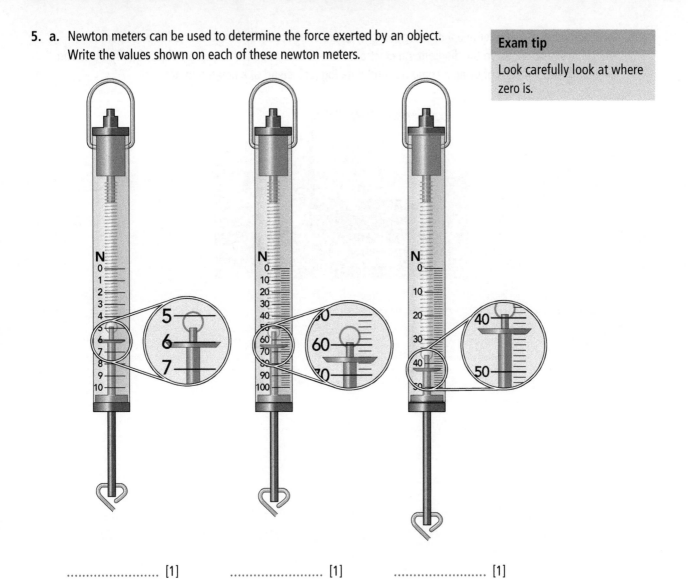

.... [1]   .... [1]   .... [1]

b. A student uses a computer and a data logger to measure and record the forces exerted in an experiment, using the set-up shown in the diagram. An electronic forcemeter was used to pull an object briefly. State and explain the advantages of using a computer and data logger instead of a newton meter.

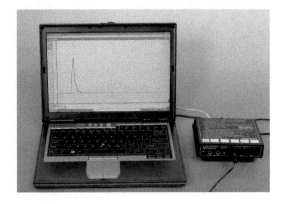

....

....

....

....

....

.... [4]

2 Measurement of small distances or short intervals of time

1. Callipers can be used to measure very small distances.

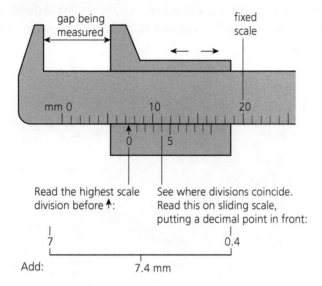

a. Use the diagram to give **one** advantage and **one** disadvantage of using callipers instead of a millimetre ruler.

....

....

....

.... [2]

b. Give **one** advantage of using digital callipers instead of standard ones.

....

.... [1]

2. A ripple tank (shown below) can be used to look at waves. A student wants to measure the distances between individual waves but finds that they move too fast to get an accurate reading of distance. They also find that the waves are really close together and are wavy. This causes a range of problems when trying to get an accurate reading of the distances between waves.

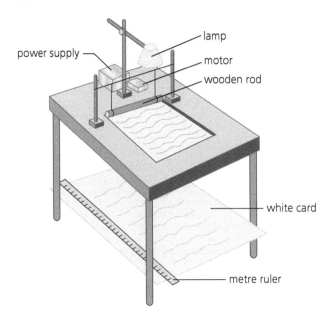

a. The waves are projected onto a large sheet of white paper next to a metre rule. The student counts the number of waves in a measured distance.

   i. The student measures 10 waves in 96 cm. Calculate the distance between each wave.

   ....

   .... [2]

   ii. Explain the advantage of measuring the number of waves in a given distance instead of trying to measure the length of each individual wave.

   ....

   ....

   .... [3]

   The method in part **a** can lead to errors and projecting the wave onto paper can cause the waves to appear diffuse.

b. A second student uses a 30 cm ruler and a camera to get a more accurate reading. Suggest how he could do this.

   ....

   ....

   ....

   .... [3]

3. The diagram shows a pendulum.

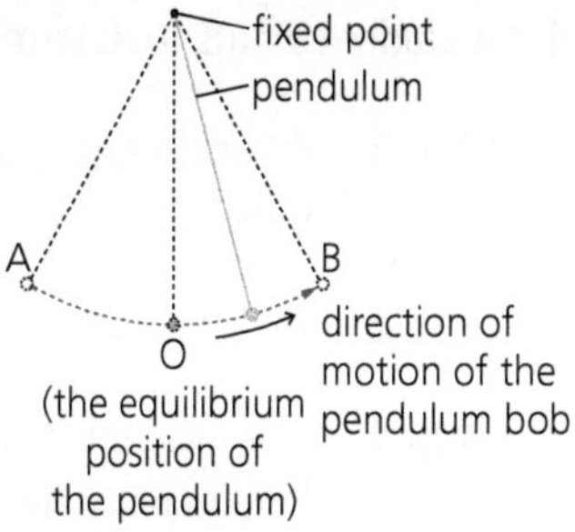

The pendulum swings from point A to point B and back again. Two students measure the time it takes and obtain very different values from each other. They both start the timer when the pendulum is released at A and stop it when they see it get to B.

fixed point
pendulum

A · B
O → direction of
(the equilibrium motion of the
position of pendulum bob
the pendulum)

Suggest an alternative method that will give a more accurate value for the time it takes for the pendulum to get from A to B. Give the advantage of this method.

....

....

....

....

.... [3]

4. A student uses light gates, as shown in the diagram, to get a very accurate reading of the time for a ball to fall.

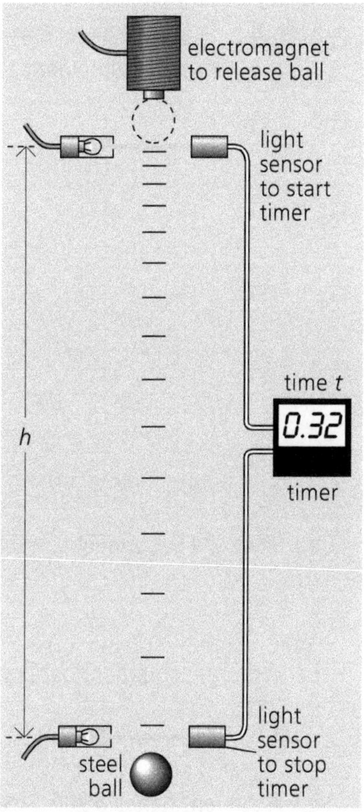

When the ball passes through the first gate it starts the timer, and when the sensor records that the ball passes the second light gate the timer stops.

electromagnet
to release ball

light
sensor
to start
timer

time t

0.32

timer

h

a. The timer shows 320 ms. Calculate the difference between 1 second and 320 ms.

....

....

.... [1]

light
sensor
to stop
timer

steel
ball

b. Suggest **four** advantages of using light gates instead of measuring the time using a stop watch.

....

....

....

....

....

.... [4]

1. A student wants to determine the extension per unit load for a spring. Here is their method.

Step 1 Attach a spring to the clamp stand by hanging it from a clamp so that it hangs freely over the side of the bench. Use a G-clamp to fix the clamp stand to the bench.

Step 2 Attach a mass hanger to the bottom of the spring with a pin positioned as shown in the diagram.

Step 3 Use a clamp to hold a metre rule vertically so that it is close to, but not touching, the spring. The pin should line up with the ruler. You will use this to measure the extension of the spring.

Step 4 Record the measurement on the ruler that the pin points to with only the mass hanger attached. Record the force as 0 N.

Step 5 Place a 1.0 N weight (100 g mass) on the mass hanger so that the spring extends. Record the measurement on the ruler that the pin now points to.

Step 6 Add another 1.0 N (100 g) mass on the mass hanger and again record the position on the ruler that the pin points to.

Step 7 Add more 1.0 N weights until a total weight of 6.0 N is hanging from the spring.

Step 8 Calculate the extension for each 100 g mass by taking the initial ruler measurement (Step 4) away from the ruler measurement at each step. Record the results in a table.

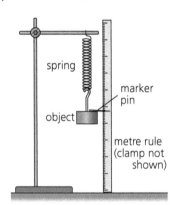

a. State the dependent variable in this experiment.

.... [1]

b. Write the equation that links mass and weight.

.... [1]

c. A student hangs a 200 g mass from a spring. Calculate the force acting on the spring. Give the unit with your answer.

(Use $g = 10$ N/kg)

....

.... [2]

d. Look at the diagram below.

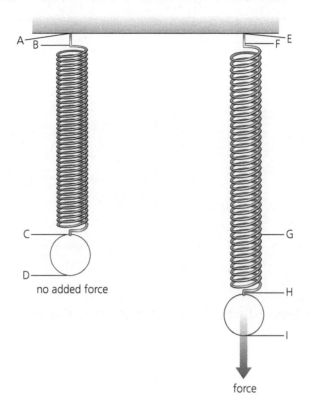

no added force

force

i. Give the letters which represent the initial length of the spring.

.... [1]

ii. Give the letters which represent the extension of the spring when loaded.

.... [1]

e. Complete the table by calculating the extension for each applied force. [1]

Force/N	Length of spring/cm	Extension of spring/cm
0	9	
1	13	
2	15	
3	17	
4	19	
5	21	
6	23	

f. Use the data in the table in part **e** to draw a graph of extension (*y*-axis) against force (*x*-axis).

[4]

g. Describe the relationship between force and extension for the spring. Give a reason for your answer.

....

....

.... [2]

h. Predict and explain what would happen to the shape of the graph if more weights were added.

....

....

.... [3]

i. Calculate the percentage change in the length of a spring with a 6 N force attached compared with an unstretched spring.

....

....

.... [3]

j. Explain how to determine the spring constant from a graph of extension against force.

....

.... [1]

k. Use your graph to calculate the spring constant, *k*, for the spring. Give the unit with your answer.

....

....

.... [3]

l. Goggles are an essential piece of safety equipment in this practical. Give a reason why.

....

.... [1]

m. Describe the function of the 'pointer' in this experiment.

....

.... [1]

n. Explain why the student measured the length of the spring and calculated the extension after the experiment.

....

.... [1]

o. In this experiment it is important to measure the length of the spring accurately. Define the term accurate.

....

.... [1]

2. A student carries out the experiment described in question 1 and draws a graph of their results.

Describe how the student could use their graph to determine the mass of an object.

....

....

....

....

....

.... [4]

3. Another student carries out the experiment described in question 1 with two different springs. Spring A is very stiff and hard to extend while spring B is easy to extend. The student draws a graph of extension (*y*-axis) against weight (*x*-axis) for each spring.

Describe and explain the differences between the two graphs.

> **Exam tip**
>
> You can use a sketch graph to help explain your answer if you wish.

....

....

....

.... [2]

4. **a.** State Hooke's law for a stretched spring.

....

.... [1]

b. When a force of 3 N is applied to a spring, the extension produced is 5 cm. Calculate the extension of the spring when a force of 12 N is applied.

....

....

....

....

....

.... [4]

5. A student is investigating the relationship between force, mass, and acceleration. They want to compare the effects of mass and force on the acceleration of a moving object.

Method A

The effect of force on the acceleration of a constant mass

chalk marks on bench at regular intervals

trolley

pulley

mass

Step 1 Set up the apparatus with five chalk lines at 20 cm intervals. The distance from the start point to the edge of the bench should be 100 cm.

Step 2 Check that the string is parallel to the bench.

Step 3 Load the mass holder with masses totalling 100 g and hold the trolley at the start point.

Step 4 Set the stopwatch to lap mode.

Step 5 Release the trolley at the same moment as starting the stopwatch.

Step 6 Press the lap timer each time the trolley passes one of the chalk lines.

Step 7 Record the times in a table.

Step 8 Repeat Steps 5 to 7 for masses of 80 g, 60 g, 40 g, and 20 g on the mass holder. To keep the mass of the system constant, you should stick the masses you remove from the holder onto the trolley.

Method B

The effect of an object's mass on its acceleration

Step 9 Use the results of experiment A to choose a suitable weight to accelerate the trolley. Load the hanger with this weight.

Step 10 Stick 100 g of masses onto the trolley using the sticky tape.

Step 11 Repeat Steps 4–7 of experiment A.

Step 12 Repeat Steps 10 and 11 another five times, increasing the mass on the trolley by 100 g each time.

a. Complete this statement using the words below.

force   mass   acceleration

An object's .... depends on the .... acting on the object and the ....
of the object. [3]

b. A trolley has a mass of 800 g. Calculate the force acting on the trolley when the acceleration is 5 m/s².

> **Exam tip**
>
> Always work in kg.

....

.... [2]

c. A student is following method A to test how force affects acceleration of a constant mass. They start with a 10 N force attached to the trolley. After each test, they remove 2 N and place the weights on the bench. Describe the error the student has made in this experiment and the effect it would have on their results.

....

....

.... [3]

d. Describe the function of the pulley in this experiment.

....

.... [1]

e. The equation force = mass × acceleration can be used to calculate the theoretical acceleration of an object. The values for acceleration measured in experiments are always lower than the values calculated using this equation. Explain why.

....

....

.... [3]

f. Give a potential source of error in method A and suggest how a student could record more accurate data without using light gates.

....

.... [2]

g. A student draws a graph of their data for method A. The trolley they use has a mass of 1.25 kg.

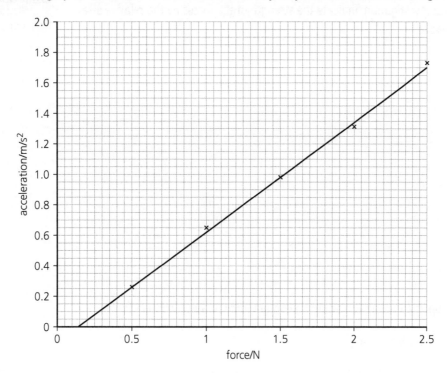

i. Calculate the theoretical acceleration when the force applied is 1.5 N. Include the unit with your answer.

....

.... [2]

ii. The student observes that the line of best fit does not go through the origin and the values they measure are always lower than the calculated theoretical acceleration. Explain the student's observations.

....

....

.... [3]

h. A student is investigating the relationship between the mass of an object and its acceleration using method B. They adapt method B by using light gates and a data logger to record the times when the trolley passes the chalk lines. Evaluate the original method B and this student's version of method B.

....

....

....

....

....

.... [4]

> **Exam tip**
>
> An 'evaluate' question wants you to give evidence for and against. This could be based on information in the question, or on your own knowledge.

i. Sketch a labelled free-body diagram to show the forces acting on the trolley in this practical investigation. Indicate the strength of the forces by the relative size of the arrows. [4]

6. A force acting upon an object can either be contact force or a non-contact force.

a. Classify the following types of force.

friction   gravity   air resistance   push   pull

Contact force	Non-contact force

[5]

b. Speed is a scalar quantity; velocity is a vector quantity. Describe the difference between a scalar and a vector quantity.

....

.... [2]

c. A student is investigating the relationship between the force acting on a system with constant mass and the acceleration. This table shows their results.

Force/N	Acceleration/m/s^2
2	0.98
4	1.92
6	2.93
8	3.92
10	4.70

i. Draw a graph of acceleration (*y*-axis) against force (*x*-axis) for the data in the table on the grid provided.

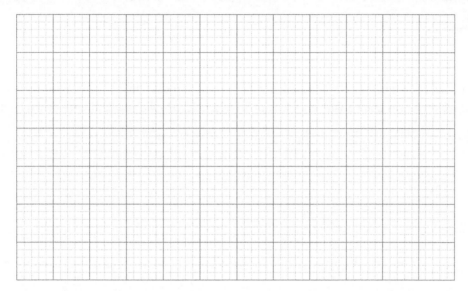

[4]

ii. Describe the relationship between applied force and acceleration shown by the graph.

.... [1]

d. Another student changes the mass but keeps the force acting on the trolley constant. This table shows their results.

Mass/kg	Acceleration/m/s^2
2	4.90
4	2.46
6	1.64
8	1.23
10	0.99

i. Draw a graph of acceleration (*y*-axis) against mass (*x*-axis) for the data in the table.

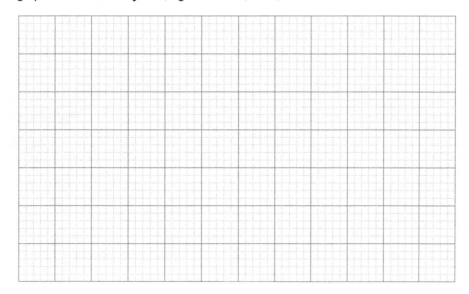

[2]

ii. Use the data to estimate a value for the force acting on the trolley.

....

.... [2]

e. A trolley of mass 1.5 kg has a force attached to the front of it. It passes point A with a velocity of 4.5 m/s. 3 seconds later it passes point B with a velocity of 5.1 m/s. Calculate the resultant force acting on the trolley.

....

....

....

....

....

.... [4]

f. A trolley starts from rest. A student uses a single light gate to record its velocity when it has travelled 30 cm from its starting position. The velocity is 3.87 m/s.

i. Rearrange the following equation to make *a* the subject.

$$v^2 - u^2 = 2as$$

....

....

.... [1]

ii. Use the equation to calculate the acceleration of the trolley.

....

....

.... [2]

iii. The trolley has a mass of 200 g. Calculate the mass attached to the trolley. Give your answer in grams.

(Use *g* = 10 N/kg)

....

....

....

....

....

....

.... [5]

> **Exam tip**
>
> You will need to use these equations:
> force = mass × acceleration
> (N)   (kg)   (m/s²)
> weight = mass × *g*
> (N)   (kg) (N/kg)
> You may need to use a combination of two equations in one question.

1. A student is investigating the relationship between the length of a wire and its resistance. The cross-section of the wire is constant.

   Here is their method.

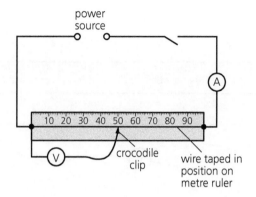

   Step 1 Set up the apparatus.

   Step 2 Set the length of the test wire to 100 cm by adjusting the positions of the crocodile clips.

   Step 3 Turn on the power supply at 1.5 V and close the switch.

   Step 4 Record the readings of voltage and current.

   Step 5 Repeat Steps 2 to 4, decreasing the length of the test wire by 20 cm each time, until the length of the wire is 20 cm.

   a. A student sets up a circuit as shown in the diagram below. Identify the error that the student has made.

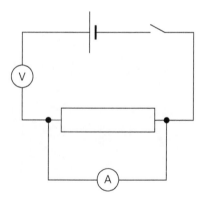

   ....

   .... [1]

   b. When the student corrects the error, the ammeter and voltmeter both read zero.

      State what they need to do to be able to take readings.

      .... [1]

   c. Complete the following sentence.

      The ammeter records the .... in the circuit and the voltmeter records

      the .... across two points in the circuit. [2]

d. The student wants to record the resistance of a 0.2 m length of wire.

On this diagram, draw an X at each point where the student should position the crocodile clips that are attached to the voltmeter.

[1]

e. A 'zero error' is often seen in this experiment. Describe a possible source of a zero error in this experiment.

....

.... [2]

f. Sketch a graph, on the axes provided, to show the results you would predict for this experiment.

[1]

g. Describe the relationship between the length of a wire and its resistance.

.... [1]

h. Complete this sentence:

If the length of a wire is doubled, then its resistance will be .... [1]

2. A student carries out the experiment described in question 1 three times for each length of wire. Their results are shown in the table.

Length of wire in cm	Resistance in ohms			
	Test 1	Test 2	Test 3	Mean
20	4.02	4.10	4.62	
40	8.24	8.36	8.97	
60	12.60	15.67	12.98	
80	16.13	16.27	16.84	
100	19.04	19.25	19.99	

a. Circle the anomalous result in the table. [1]

b. Calculate the mean resistance for each length of wire and complete the table.

....

....

....

.... [3]

Exam tip

Remember not to include any anomalous results when calculating a mean.

c. The student does not allow the wire to cool down between each repeat experiment.
Explain the effect this has on the repeatability of the student's results.

....

....

.... [3]

Exam tip

You should quote examples from the results in your answer.

d. Use the data in the table to plot a graph of mean resistance in ohms against length of wire in centimetres. Draw a line of best fit on your graph.

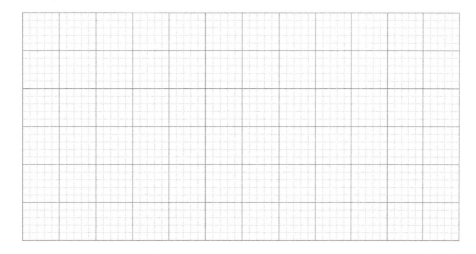

[4]

e. The student now wants to investigate the relationship between the cross-section of a wire and its resistance. Suggest what happens to the resistance of a wire if the cross-sectional area is doubled.

....

....

.... [2]

f. A variable resistor is often used in this experiment to keep the current below 1.0 A. Explain why the resistance of a wire will increase if the circuit is left on for a long time with a high current flowing.

....

....

....

....

.... [4]

1. A student is investigating the reflection and refraction of light as it passes through a rectangular glass block.

   This is their method.

   Step 1   Place the glass block in the centre of a piece of paper (landscape view) and draw round it.

   Step 2   Remove the block and draw a dotted normal line at right angles to the edge of one long side of the block, about halfway along.

   Step 3   Draw a line to represent the incident ray at 30° to the normal.

   Step 4   Place the block back onto the rectangle drawn on the paper.

   Step 5   Switch on a ray box with a narrow slit in front of the bulb and shine a light along the path of the incident ray. (Caution: the ray box may get hot.)

   Step 6   Observe the path of the light through the block and out of the other side.

   Step 7   Mark the path of the emergent light ray on the other side of the block with a pencil line. Also mark the path of the reflected ray.

   Step 8   Remove the glass block. Draw a normal at the point where the light emerged from the glass block.

   Step 9   Draw a line to join the incident and emergent rays through the rectangle representing the glass block. This gives the path of the refracted ray.

   Step 10 Measure the angle between the incident ray and the normal and between the refracted ray and the normal using a protractor. Record your results in a table.

   Step 11 Repeat for other angles of incidence. State the relationship between the emergent ray and the incident ray.

   a. The student carries out this experiment. Their drawing is shown below.

   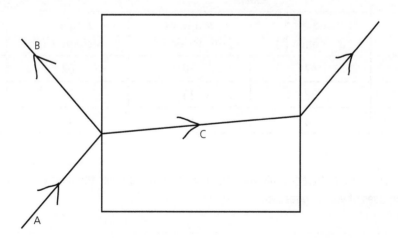

   i. Draw **two** lines on the figure to show where the student should draw the normal lines.   [2]

ii. Three rays are labelled **A, B,** and **C**. Give the name of each ray.

....

....

.... [3]

iii. Complete this sentence to give the student's answer to Step 11.

The emergent ray is .... to the incident ray. [1]

b. Describe **two** possible sources of error in this experiment.

....

.... [2]

c. Describe what would happen to the beam of light if it hit the block at an angle of 90° to the surface.

....

.... [2]

d. Suggest an alternative type of wave that could be used to investigate reflection or refraction.

.... [1]

2. A student is comparing refraction by two different materials, using the method given in question 1. Her data is shown in the table.

Repeat	Glass		Perspex	
	Angle of incidence (°)	Angle of refraction (°)	Angle of incidence (°)	Angle of refraction (°)
1	47	30	62	36
2	38	24	51	31
3	28	18	41	26

[3]

a. Suggest a way in which the student could alter her investigation to make the data easier to interpret. Give **two** advantages of your suggestion.

....

....

.... [3]

b. Give an advantage of measuring the angles of incidence and refraction at three different points on the surface of each block instead of one.

.... [1]

5 Measured quantities such as angles of refraction and reflection

c. Describe what happens to light when it is refracted.

....
.... [2]

d. Explain why light is refracted.

....
....
....
....
....
....
....
.... [5]

Exam tip

Pay close attention to the command words used in each part of the question. Remember that 'describe' means that you should say *what* is happening. 'Explain' means that you need to say *why* something is happening.

e. State **one** factor that determines the amount of refraction that occurs when light passes from one material to another.

....
.... [1]

f. Suggest whether light travels more slowly in glass or Perspex. Explain your answer using data from the table. Explain how you decide.

....
....
.... [3]

g. Describe what happens to a light ray in the glass when the angle of incidence is greater than the critical angle.

....
....
....
.... [3]

3. Instead of carrying out the practical investigation described in question 2 in a laboratory, it can be carried out as an online simulation. Evaluate the use of simulations in physics.

....

....

....

....

....

....

....

....

....

....

....

.... [6]

Exam tip

For an 'evaluate' question you need to give both advantages and disadvantages. You should give your opinion and justify it.

Sometimes a planning table can help you to structure a balanced answer.

	Simulations	Hands-on practical
advantages		
disadvantages		

5 Measured quantities such as angles of refraction and reflection

4. A student is investigating reflection of light by a plane mirror. They position a ray box to produce a beam of light with an angle of incidence of 65°.

   a. Draw an accurate diagram to show what the student observes.

[5]

The student then investigates refraction by a rectangular block of glass. They position a ray box to produce a beam of light with an angle of incidence of 35°. They find that the angle of refraction is 22°.

b. i. Draw an accurate diagram to show the student's results.

[3]

   ii. Calculate the refractive index of the glass.

....
....
....
....[2]

6 Comparing derived quantities such as density

1. A student is investigating the density of a regularly shaped object, an irregularly shaped object, and a liquid.

    A: Density of a solid (in the shape of a cube or cuboid)

    Step 1   Measure and record the mass of the solid.

    Step 2   Measure and record the length, width, and height of the solid.

    B: Density of a solid (irregularly shaped object)

    Step 1   Measure and record the mass of the object.

    Step 2   Add water to a measuring cylinder until it is half-full. (There needs to be enough water so that when you put the solid into the water, the water will cover the solid but will not rise above the top of the measuring scale.)

    Step 3   With your eye level with the water's surface, measure the volume of water and record the value.

    Step 4   Carefully place the solid object into the measuring cylinder.

    Step 5   Measure and record the new volume of the water.

    C: Density of a liquid

    Step 1   Record the type of liquid whose density you are measuring.

    Step 2   Measure and record the mass of an empty measuring cylinder.

    Step 3   Pour the liquid into the measuring cylinder, making sure it does not go above the top of the cylinder's measuring scale.

    Step 4   Measure and record the mass of the cylinder with the liquid in it. Work out the mass of the liquid in the measuring cylinder.

    Step 5   Measure and record the volume of liquid in the cylinder.

    a. List the equipment needed to carry out parts A, B, and C of this investigation.

    ....

    ....

    ....

    ....

    ....

    ....

    ....

    .... [6]

b. For each of these objects, suggest the best method for finding the density.

  i. pebble

  .... [1]

  ii. textbook

  .... [1]

  iii. block of modelling clay

  .... [1]

c. When an object is placed into the measuring cylinder, the water level rises. State what the increase in volume of water is equal to.

.... [1]

d. Suggest why it is important that an object is completely submerged before measuring the new volume of water.

....

.... [1]

e. Describe **three** sources of error when carrying out an experiment to find the density of an irregularly shaped object.

....

....

....

.... [3]

f. A block of clay is found to have a volume of 50 cm³ and a mass of 65 g.

  i. Write the equation that links density, mass, and volume.

  .... [1]

  ii. Calculate the density of the clay. Give your answer in kg/m³.

  ....

  ....

Exam tip
There are 1 000 000 cm³ in 1 m³. Always check whether you need to convert any units before substituting them into an equation.

....

.... [3]

g. The student then considers a regularly shaped object.

  i. Calculate the volume of a cube with sides of length 0.5 m, giving your answer in cm³.

  ....

  .... [2]

ii. The block has a density of 4.2 g/cm³. Calculate the mass of the block, giving your answer in kg.

....

....

....

.... [3]

h. 100 ml of water has a mass of 100 g. 60 ml of honey has a mass of 87 g. Compare the densities of water and honey.

....

....

....

> **Exam tip**
>
> The command word 'compare' tells you that you need to say which value is greater or which is smaller.

....

.... [3]

2. A chess piece is carved from a cylinder of wood with a diameter of 4 cm and a height of 5 cm.

a. Calculate the volume of the cylinder of wood. Give your answer in cm³ to 2 significant figures.

(Volume of a cylinder = $\pi r^2 h$).

....

.... [2]

b. Describe how you could use the apparatus shown below to find out the volume of wood removed from the cylinder when carving the chess piece.

....

....

....

....

....

....

....

.... [6]

6 Comparing derived quantities such as density

c. A student weighs the cylinder before and after it is carved. Its mass is 44 g before carving and 33 g after it is carved. Use your answer to part **a** to calculate the volume of the chess piece.

....

....

....

....

.... [3]

Exam tip

You will need to use the equation you wrote in question 1 part f.i

d. An irregularly shaped object has a recorded mass of 5.47 g. The displays of three balances are shown below. Choose the balance which would be most appropriate to check the accuracy of the recorded mass. Justify your answer.

A	B	C
000.0 g	00.00 g	0.000 g

....

....

.... [2]

3. A student wants to identify an unknown liquid in a bottle. Table A shows the data that the student records. Table B shows the densities of some common liquids. Determine which of the liquids in Table B is most likely to be the unknown sample.

Table A

Mass of empty measuring cylinder	64.6 g
Mass of measuring cylinder with unknown liquid	142.8 g
Volume of unknown liquid	85 cm³

Table B

Liquid	Density/g/cm³
acetone	0.79
olive oil	0.92
petroleum	0.69
turpentine	0.87
water	1.00

....

....

.... [3]

1. A student is investigating the emission of infrared radiation by silver and black cans. Here is their method.

   Step 1 Place two drinks cans (one painted silver and one painted matt black) on a heatproof mat. Beakers with aluminium foil lids can be used as an alternative.

   Step 2 Carefully pour 150 ml of hot water into each of the two cans using a measuring cylinder.

   Step 3 If you are using beakers, place the lids onto the beakers.

   Step 4 Put a thermometer into the water in each container.

   Step 5 Start the stopwatch, and record the temperature of the water in the two containers every 60 s for 5 minutes.

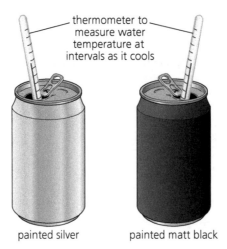

thermometer to measure water temperature at intervals as it cools

painted silver   painted matt black

   a. Describe **three** variables that should be controlled in this experiment.

   ....

   ....

   ....

   .... [3]

   b. Use the results in the table to identify which can is the best emitter of infrared radiation. Give a reason for your choice.

Time/seconds	Temperature of water/°C	
	Silver can	Matt black can
0	98	98
60	90	85
120	83	74
180	75	64
240	68	55
300	62	49

   ....

   ....

   ....

   .... [2]

c. Calculate the average rate of change of temperature for each can in °C/s.

....

....

....

.... [4]

d. **i.** Plot a graph of temperature against time for the silver can.

[3]

ii. Use your graph to estimate the rate of change of the water temperature at 150 s.

....

.... [2]

e. The student also has an infrared lamp available. Describe how the student would use this equipment to investigate which can is the best absorber of infrared radiation.

....

....

....

....

....

.... [6]

f. In this experiment, a data logger can be used instead of a thermometer. Explain the advantages of using a data logger.

....

....

....

.... [3]

2. A student plans an experiment to measure the amount of infrared radiation emitted from different surfaces using the apparatus shown below.

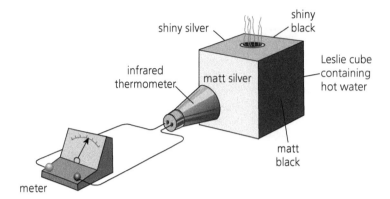

This is their method.

Step 1   Place the Leslie cube on a heatproof mat and fill it with hot water. Take care as you do this.

Step 2   Use an infrared thermometer/detector to measure the amount of infrared radiation emitted from one surface of the Leslie cube.

Step 3   Carefully rotate the Leslie cube and measure the amount of infrared radiation emitted from each of the surfaces in turn.

Step 4   Record your results in a suitable table.

a. State **one** control variable in this experiment.

.... [1]

b. Name the independent variable in this experiment.

.... [1]

c. A student measured the infrared radiation from the four different surfaces using the infrared detector. Their results are shown in the table. Plot a bar chart for this data on the grid provided.

Surface	Infrared radiation/units
shiny silver	17
matt silver	35
shiny black	39
matt black	47

Exam tip

Some tables and graphs have variables that are given in 'units' or in 'arbitrary units'. If you see this in an exam, don't panic – they are just used to show a general trend, or values when the actual units are not needed.

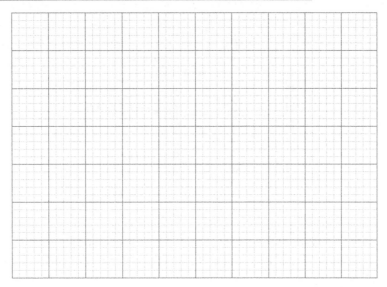

[4]

d. The student's hypothesis was:

'The colour of the surface will affect emission of infrared radiation more than the roughness of the surface.'

Write a conclusion based on the student's results and their hypothesis.

Exam tip

If you are asked to write a conclusion, always quote data to back up what you are saying.

....

....

....

....

....

.... [4]

e. Predict which surface would be the best absorber and which surface would be the poorest absorber of infrared radiation. Give reasons for your answers.

....

....

....

.... [4]

3. A student is investigating the effectiveness of different types of materials as thermal insulators.

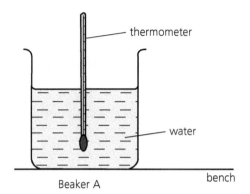

Beaker A

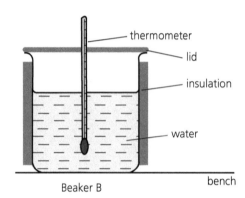

Beaker B

Step 1 Set up the containers as shown. Leave one container unwrapped. Wrap each of the other containers in a different material using elastic bands or tape to hold the material in place. Try to use the same thickness of each material.

Step 2 Prepare lids for the containers from the same material as the wrapping, or made from aluminium foil or cling film.

Step 3 Make a hole in each lid that is just big enough for a thermometer to fit through.

Step 4 Use a measuring cylinder to pour equal amounts of hot water into each container.

Step 5 Put the lids onto the containers and insert a thermometer through each lid so that it rests near the bottom of the water.

Step 6 Start the stopwatch and measure the initial temperature of the water.

Step 7 Every three minutes for 15 minutes, use the thermometer to gently stir the water and then measure and record the temperature of the water in each beaker.

a. Describe what happens to the thermal energy of the water as its temperature falls.

.... [1]

b. Give the function of each of the following pieces of equipment in this practical.

   i. lid

   .... [1]

   ii. measuring cylinder

   .... [1]

   iii. thermometer

   .... [1]

c. Describe **two** advantages of using a data logger instead of a thermometer to measure the temperature.

....

.... [2]

d. One control variable for this experiment is the volume of water added into the beaker. Suggest a suitable piece of equipment to accurately measure the volume of water.

.... [1]

e. Two students want to plot their data on graphs. For each student, explain what type of graph they should draw:

   i. for plotting every point and comparing the slopes

   ....

   .... [2]

   ii. for plotting the temperature change for each material.

   ....

   .... [2]

f. 0.8 kg of water is used in the experiment and left to cool.
The initial temperature of the water is 84 °C. The final temperature is 61 °C.

   i. Calculate the energy transferred during the five-minute period.

   The specific heat capacity of water is 4.2 J/kg °C.

   ....

   ....

   .... [2]

   ii. Calculate the percentage change in the temperature of the water over the five-minute period.

   ....

   ....

   .... [2]

g. A student carries out this experiment and records the following data. Calculate the temperature of the water after 1 hour.

Exam tip

Make sure you look carefully at the units of the data given.

Room temperature	Starting temperature	Average rate of cooling	Temperature after one hour
25 °C	65 °C	0.9 °C/minute	

....

....

.... [3]

4. A student is investigating the effect of using different thicknesses of bubble wrap as a thermal insulator. Bubble wrap can be popped. They wrap a beaker in 10 layers of unpopped bubble wrap and then wrap a second beaker in 1 layer of popped bubble wrap. Both beakers contain the same volume of water at the same initial temperature. The water is left to cool and the student measures and records the temperature every minute for 10 minutes.

a. Predict the results of this experiment.

....

....

....

....

....

.... [4]

5. A student carries out an experiment to test how effective cardboard is an insulator. The table shows their data.

Time/minutes	Temperature/°C
0	90
5	77
10	65
15	55
20	46
25	39
30	33
35	29
40	26
45	24
50	24

a. Draw a graph on the grid provided to show the data in the table.

[4]

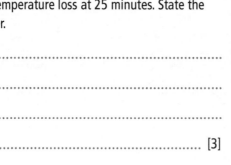

b. Estimate the rate of temperature loss at 25 minutes. State the units with your answer.

....

....

....

.... [3]

6. A group of students is investigating the effectiveness of different materials as thermal insulators, but have trouble comparing their results and analysing the data, which is shown in the table.

Temperature/°C	No insulation	Newspaper	Bubble wrap	Cotton wool
0	89	72	92	68
5	81	65	86	64
10	74	58	80	60
15	67	62	75	56
20	61	46	71	53
25	56	41	66	50
30	51	36	62	47

a. Bethany thinks that the bubble wrap was the best insulator while Aimee thinks that the cotton wool was the best insulator. Explain who is correct.

....

....

....

....

.... [3]

Exam tip

This is a question about analysis of data, so use data in your answer!

b. Look at the data in the table. Suggest what the students could do to make the results more comparable.

....

....

....

.... [2]

7. The specific heat capacity of a material can be determined using the method below.

Step 1 Find the mass of a block of the material.

Step 2 Place the block on an insulating mat.

Step 3 With the power supply switched off, set up the apparatus as shown.

Step 4 Place the thermometer in the hole in the block along with a small amount of water and measure the temperature. Record this as the 'starting temperature' of the block.

Step 5 Switch the power supply on and start the stopwatch.

Step 6 Record the current and potential difference.

Step 7 Watch the reading on the thermometer. Record the temperature every 60 seconds for ten minutes.

Step 8 When the temperature reaches 15 °C above the starting temperature, switch off the power supply and stop the stopwatch.

Step 9 Record the thermometer reading and the time on the stopwatch.

a. To record the current and potential difference, a circuit needs to be set up that includes an ammeter and a voltmeter. Which **two** of these statements best describe how they should be connected?

An ammeter should be connected in series. ☐
An ammeter should be connected in parallel. ☐
A voltmeter should be connected in series. ☐
A voltmeter should be connected in parallel. ☐ [2]

b. Two students carry out the experiment using identical blocks. One student insulated the block with polystyrene while the other student did not use insulation. Both students used their data to draw graphs and to calculate the specific heat capacity of the blocks they were testing.

Suggest which student would have more accurate results. Explain why there would be a difference in their results.

....

....

....

....

....

....

.... [6]

c. A student is investigating the specific heat capacity of bronze. They measure how many seconds it takes for the temperature of the block to increase by 1 °C.

Explain how the student can make their measurement more accurate.

....

....

.... [2]

d. Explain why water is put into the hole with the thermometer.

....

....

.... [2]

e. Use the data in the table below to predict which metal will take the longest time for the temperature of a block of the same mass to rise by 30 °C.

Metal	Specific heat capacity/J/kg °C
copper	385
steel	452
aluminium	913

Explain your answer.

....

....

.... [2]

f. Instead of using a thermometer to measure the temperature, an alternative would be to use a temperature probe with a data-logger.

i. Give **two** advantages of using a data-logger.

....

....

.... [2]

ii. Suggest **one** disadvantage of using a data-logger.

....

.... [1]

g. A student carries out the investigation on an unknown metal and records the following data.

Time/s	Temperature/°C	Work done/kJ
0	21	0
60	22	1.8
120	24	3.6
180	28	5.4
240	32	7.2
300	36	9
360	40	10.8
420	44	12.6
480	48	14.4
540	52	16.2
600	56	18

i. Draw a graph of the data and then use the data in the table in part **e** and your graph to determine the identity of the metal.

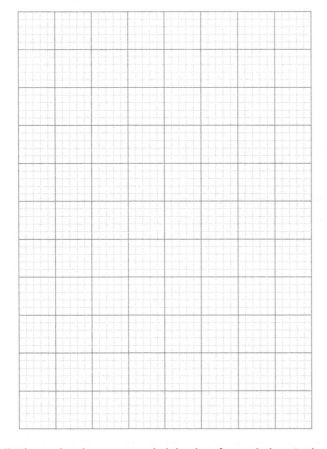

Exam tip

The data for work done transferred in the table is in kJ, but the standard unit for work done is J. You can draw your graph in kJ but be careful when you do the calculation.

[6]

ii. The student has not recorded the data for work done in the best way. State how the data should have been recorded differently and explain why this change is important.

....

....

Exam tip

It's not the units.

.... [2]

h. A second student carries out this investigation and draws a graph of his results. He notices that the first part of the graph is curved. The curve is followed by a straight section. Suggest a reason why the first part of the graph is curved.

....

....

.... [2]

8. A student uses the equipment shown to heat a block of copper of unknown mass. Use the data given below to calculate the mass of the block. Give your answer to an appropriate number of significant figures.

Current in circuit = 1.2 A

Potential difference in the circuit = 12 V

Temperature change at 4 minutes = 8 °C

Specific heat capacity of copper = 385 J/kg °C

Exam tip

You will need to use these equations:
power (W) = current (A) × potential difference (V)
energy transferred (J) = power (W) × time (s)
energy transferred (J) = mass (kg) × specific heat capacity (J/kg/°C) × change in temperature (°C)

....

....

....

....

....

....

.... [6]

1. Here are two ways in which oscillations can be measured.

   (a)

   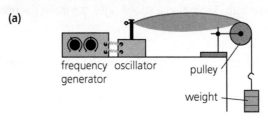

   (b)

   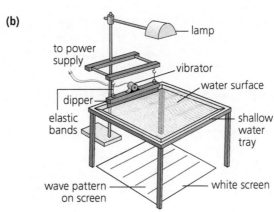

Method A   Wave behaviour in a solid

Step 1   Assemble the apparatus as shown in Figure a.

Step 2   Measure the length of string between the vibration generator and the pulley.

Step 3   Turn on the signal generator.

Step 4   Increase the frequency of the vibration from zero until you can see one complete wave on the string.

Step 5   Record the frequency of the signal generator.

Step 6   Continue to increase the frequency until you see a second wave pattern, with two complete waves.

Step 7   Record the frequency on the signal generator.

Step 8   Continue this process to find the frequencies which form three and four complete waves on the string.

Method B   Wave behaviour in a liquid

Step 1   Set up the ripple tank as shown in Figure b.

Step 2   Fill the tray with water to a depth of about 1 cm. The dipper should just touch the surface of the water.

Step 3   Place the lamp so that it shines into the tray.

Step 4   Turn on the power supply and lower the speed of the motor until separate waves are clearly visible on the white screen below.

Step 5   Measure the distance between the two visible waves that are furthest apart on the screen. Divide this distance by the number of waves visible to calculate the wavelength.

Step 6   Count the number of waves passing a fixed point in 10 seconds. Divide this number by 10 to find the frequency of the waves.

A student is investigating water waves in a ripple tank. When using a ripple tank, the wave may travel very quickly which makes it difficult to measure the wavelength. Setting up a strobe light can make the waves appear stationary and make them easier to count and measure.

a. Suggest an alternative way to measure the wavelength accurately that does not involve a strobe light.

....

....

....

.... [3]

b. Explain the function of the white screen and the lamp used in Method B.

....

....

.... [2]

c. Using the ripple tank, a student counted 22 waves passing a fixed point in 5.0 seconds. Calculate the frequency of the waves in the ripple tank in Hz.

....

....

.... [2]

d. An important part of this practical is making accurate measurements. For the waves in the ripple tank, describe how you can use appropriate apparatus to measure

i. the wavelength

....

....

.... [2]

ii. the frequency.

....

....

.... [2]

Two students carry out an experiment to measure waves in a ripple tank.

Student A measures the wavelength of a single wave.

Student B measures the wavelength of ten waves and then divides the value by 10.

e. Explain which student's data will be more accurate. Give a reason for your answer.

....

....

....

.... [3]

f. Give **one** advantage of using a wave generator or a motor to produce waves in a ripple tank, instead of producing them by hand.

.... [1]

g. State the equation that links wave speed, frequency and wavelength.

.... [1]

Exam tip

This is a slightly different experiment because the waves are forming circles rather than straight lines. Don't be put off by the slight difference – the theory is exactly the same!

h. A student uses a wave generator to produce waves that radiate out in a circle. Describe how the student can estimate the speed of these waves as accurately as possible.

....

....

....

....

....

....

....

....

.... [6]

i. The student counted 17 waves passing a fixed point in 11 seconds. They counted 10 waves in 50 cm. Calculate the speed of the waves. Give the unit with your answer.

....

....

....

....

.... [3]

2. A student sets up the apparatus shown to investigate waves on a string.

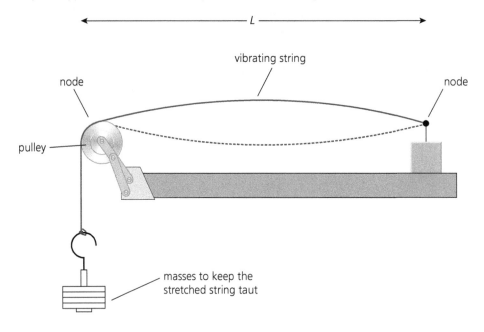

a. The student is unable to observe a complete wave. Describe how the student can calculate the wavelength.

....

....

.... [2]

b. Suggest how this equipment can be altered to change the wavelength of the wave generated.

....

....

....

.... [3]

c. A wave has a frequency of 5.6 kHz and a speed of 5100 m/s. Calculate the wavelength of the wave.

Exam tip

You need to use the equation that links wave speed, frequency and wavelength.

....

....

....

.... [2]

1. A student is investigating resistance in series and parallel circuits. They use the following method.

    Step 1 Set up two resistors in series as shown in Figure a.

    Step 2 Close the switch and record readings of voltage and current for the series circuit.

    Step 3 Set up the two resistors in parallel as shown in Figure b.

    Step 4 Close the switch and record readings of voltage and current for the parallel circuit.

(a)
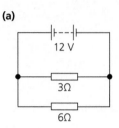

(b)
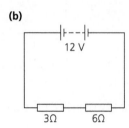

    a. Calculate the total resistance in the series circuit.

    .... [1]

    b. Explain why the resistance in the parallel circuit will be lower than the value calculated in part **a**.

    ....

    ....

    ....

    .... [3]

    c. A series circuit was set up and run for 3 minutes. During this time, 45 J of energy was transferred and the charge transferred was 9 C. Calculate the resistance in the circuit.

    ....

    ....

    ....

    ....

    ....

    ....

    ....

    ....

    ....

    .... [6]

Exam tip

You need to use these equations:

charge = current × time

energy transferred = p.d. × current × time

p.d. = resistance × current

2. A student is investigating the relationship between the potential difference across a component and the current flowing through it. Here is their method.

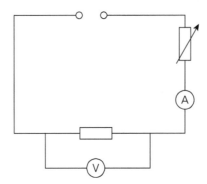

Step 1 With the power supply switched off, set up the circuit shown.

Step 2 Adjust the variable resistor and measure the current and potential difference for your component. Do not allow the current to go above 1.0 A.

Step 3 Starting with the variable resistor at its lowest resistance (so that the current is at its highest), measure the current and potential difference for your component.

Step 4 Switch off the power supply.

Step 5 Increase the resistance of the variable resistor in about six steps between the minimum and maximum resistances, and each time measure the current and potential difference for the component. Switch off the power supply between readings.

Step 6 Reverse the polarity of the power pack, by swapping the positive and negative connections, and repeat Steps 1–5.

Step 7 Repeat the experiment for each component you are testing. When testing a diode, you should insert a fixed resistor in series with the diode, and swap the ammeter for a milliammeter.

a. Describe and explain **three** health and safety concerns a student might need to be aware of during this practical.

> **Exam tip**
>
> This question is worth 6 marks, so there are 2 marks for each point. You need to explain how you will reduce each risk that you describe.

....

....

....

....

....

....

....

....

.... [6]

b. Draw a line from each circuit symbol to its name.

Battery

Cell

Diode

Filament lamp

Thermistor

Variable resistor

[4]

c. Sketch the current–potential difference graph for a filament lamp.

> **Exam tip**
>
> When 'sketch' is the command word, you need to show the axes, the shape of the graph, and any coordinates where the line crosses the axes (if relevant). Sometimes the axes will be provided. You don't need a scale on the axes in a sketch graph.

[3]

d. Describe and explain the shape of the current–potential difference graph for a filament lamp.

....

....

....

....

.... [4]

e. A student investigates the *I–V* characteristics of two unknown components. Their results are shown below.

Potential difference/V	Current in component 1/A	Current in component 2/A
−3.0	−0.14	0.00
−2.0	−0.12	0.00
−1.0	−0.05	0.00
0.0	0.00	0.00
1.0	0.05	0.01
2.0	0.11	0.18
3.0	0.15	0.40

i. Plot graphs of current against potential difference for components 1 and 2 on the graph paper provided.

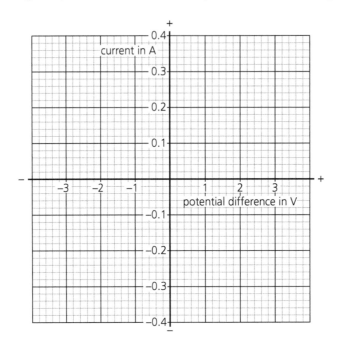

[2]

ii. Identify the two components, 1 and 2.

1 ....

2 .... [2]

iii. Compare and explain the shapes of the current–potential difference graphs for the two components.

....

....

....

....

....

....

.... [6]

iv. Use your graph from part **e.i.** to predict the current through component 1 when the potential difference across it is 4.0 V.

.... [1]

v. Use the graph for component 1 to find its resistance.

....

....

....

.... [3]

f. In this experiment, describe the purpose of reversing the battery.

....

....

.... [2]

g. Suggest why a milliammeter is used instead of an ammeter when measuring the current flowing through a diode.

.... [1]

2. Fixed resistors follow Ohm's law, which states that current and voltage are directly proportional. A student carries out two experiments to measure the current and potential difference for a fixed resistor. Their results are recorded in the table. Complete the table by adding the voltage for Test 2.

> **Exam tip**
>
> You don't need to know the resistance to be able to answer this question – you can use ratios.

a.

	Test 1	Test 2
Current/A	14.8	9.2
Potential difference/V	7.4	

[2]

b. Give a reason why the line of best fit for a graph of current against potential difference for a fixed resistor should go through the origin.

.... [1]

c. A student is investigating the current and potential difference across a fixed 5 Ω resistor. Calculate the current flowing in the resistor when the potential difference is 2 V.

....

....

.... [2]

1. A student uses the following set-up to find the focal length of a lens.

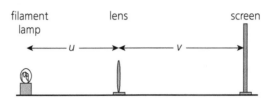

   a. State what u and v represent.

   ....

   .... [2]

   b. Show, on the diagram, where a student should place an object to be illuminated.   [1]

   c. Describe how a student could use the set-up to determine the focal length of the lens.

   ....

   ....

   ....

   ....

   ....

   ....

   .... [6]

   d. Describe **two** sources of error in this experiment.

   ....

   ....

   .... [2]

2. A student is investigating the transmission of light through three different materials, as shown in the diagram.

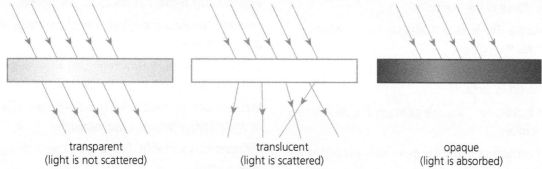

transparent	translucent	opaque
(light is not scattered)	(light is scattered)	(light is absorbed)

a. Suggest a piece of equipment that could accurately measure the transmission of light.

.... [1]

b. Suggest **one** independent variable for this experiment.

.... [1]

c. A student wants to measure the transmission of light but finds that using a filament lamp gives out light that is too diffuse. Suggest an alternative way of producing a suitable beam of light.

.... [1]

Acceleration Increase in velocity per second

Accurate Close to the true value

Air resistance The force that opposes motion when an object moves through air

Ammeter An electrical instrument used to measure electric current in amperes

Angle of incidence The angle between the incident ray and the normal

Angle of reflection The angle between the reflected ray and the normal

Angle of refraction The angle between the refracted ray and the normal

Anomalous result A data value that does not fit the pattern of the other values

Callipers An instrument used to measure the dimensions of an object with precision

Conductor A material that is able to easily pass on thermal or electrical energy

Control variable A factor that is kept constant during an experiment

Current The rate of flow of charged particles such as electrons or ions in a circuit; it is measured in amperes (A), where 1 ampere is a rate of flow of charge of 1 coulomb per second

Current–potential difference graph A graph of current flowing through a component against the potential difference across it which can be used to find the resistance of the component

Data logger An electronic device that automatically records the results of an experiment over time

Density The mass per unit volume of an object, measured in kilograms per cubic metre (kg/m³)

Dependent variable The variable being measured or tested in an experiment

Emergent ray The light that comes out after being reflected by a mirror or after passing through a lens or a medium such as glass or water

Estimate An approximate calculation or judgement of the value of a quantity

Extension An increase in length

Filament lamp A bulb containing a piece of wire that glows when a current is passed through it

Force A push or a pull exerted on an object

Free-body diagram A diagram that uses arrows to model the relative sizes and directions of the forces acting on an object

Frequency The number of waves passing a point per second or the number of vibrations per second

Friction The force acting between two surfaces that opposes motion

Gravity A force that attracts an object towards another body with mass, such as the Earth

Incident ray The light arriving at the surface of a mirror or the boundary between two materials

Independent variable The variable that is changed in an experiment

Infrared radiation The part of the electromagnetic radiation just beyond the red part of the visible spectrum; it can be detected by its heating effect

Leslie cube A metal cube with four different types of surface: shiny silver, matt white, shiny black and matt black

Light gates A sensor that detects when an object passes through it which can be connected to a data logger to measure and record the speed of an object and the time taken between two light gates

Line of best fit A straight line or curve drawn on a graph that represents the trend of the data points

Mass A measure of the amount of matter in an object, measured in kilograms (kg)

Newton meter An instrument used to measure force

Normal line A construction line lying at right angles to a boundary between two materials or to the surface of a mirror

Observations Measurements or other information recorded during an experiment

Ohm's law The current in a resistor at constant temperature is proportional to the potential difference across the resistor; the resistance does not depend on the current or the potential difference

Opaque Not able to be seen through; not transparent

Parallel Two lines that have the same continuous distance between them; in a circuit, when components are connected across each other

Perspex A solid transparent type of plastic

Potential difference (p.d.) The work done on a coulomb of charge between two points in a circuit

Pull A force that causes or attempts to cause movement towards its source

Pulley A wheel on an axle over which a rope or chain passes in order to lift heavy objects more easily

Push A force that moves or attempts to move an object away from its source

Reflection The return of waves after they hit a surface

Refraction The change of direction of waves when they travel across a boundary where their speed changes

Refractive index speed of light in air ÷ speed of light in a substance; symbol *n*

Reliable Data that is complete and accurate

Resistance Potential difference across a component ÷ the current through it, measured in ohms (Ω)

Ripple tank A shallow glass tank of water used to demonstrate the properties of waves

Scalar quantity A quantity such as mass that has a size (magnitude) but not a direction

Series Components that are connected into a circuit next to each other

Specific heat capacity The energy needed to raise the temperature of 1 kg of a substance by 1°C

Theoretical Results that have been obtained using logic rather than by experiments

Thermal energy The energy transferred from a hotter object to a colder object

Thermometer An instrument used to measure temperature

Translucent A material that allows light to pass through it but which diffuses the light so that an object seen through the material is not clear

Transparent A material that allows light to pass through it

Vector quantity A quantity such as velocity that has direction as well as size (magnitude)

Velocity The speed in a given direction, measured in metres per second (m/s)

Voltmeter An electrical instrument used to measure e.m.f. or potential difference (i.e. voltage) in volts

Zero error When a measuring device does not read zero when it should so that all measurements are either too high or too low

In most cases, the equations below are given in both word and symbol form.

$g = 9.8$ N/kg (Earth's gravitational field strength)

    $= 9.8$ m/s^2 (acceleration of free fall)

You may be asked to use 10 N/kg for g.

Density, mass and volume

$$\text{density} = \frac{\text{mass}}{\text{volume}}$$

$$\rho = \frac{m}{v}$$

Speed

$$\text{average speed} = \frac{\text{distance moved}}{\text{time taken}}$$

$$v = \frac{s}{t}$$

Acceleration

$$\text{average speed} = \frac{\text{change in velocity}}{\text{time taken}}$$

$$a = \frac{v - u}{t}$$

Force, mass and acceleration

force = mass × acceleration

$$F = ma$$

Momentum

momentum = mass × velocity

Impulse

impulse = force × time = change in momentum

Weight

weight = mass × g

$$W = mg$$

Moment of a force

moment of a force = force ×   perpendicular
   about a point   distance from point

Hooke's law for a stretched spring

applied force = spring constant × extension

$$F = kx$$

Pressure and force

$$\text{pressure} = \frac{\text{force}}{\text{area}}$$

$$\rho = \frac{F}{A}$$

Pressure in a liquid

pressure = density × g × depth

$$p = \rho gh$$

Work

work done = force × distance moved in direction of force

$$W = Fd$$

Gravitational potential energy

gravitational potential energy = mass × g × height

$$PE = mgh$$

Kinetic energy

$$\text{kinetic energy} = \frac{1}{2} \times \text{mass} \times \text{velocity}^2$$

$$KE = \frac{1}{2}mv^2$$

Energy and temperature change

energy transferred = mass × specific heat capacity × temperature change

$$E = mc\Delta T$$

Energy and state change

energy transferred = mass × specific latent heat

$$E = mL$$

Waves

speed = frequency × wavelength

$$v = f\lambda$$

Refraction of light

$$\text{refractive index} = \frac{\text{sine of angle of incidence}}{\text{sine of angle of refraction}}$$

$$n = \frac{\sin i}{\sin r}$$

Total internal reflection

$$\text{sine of critical angle} = \frac{1}{\text{refractive index}}$$

$$\sin c = \frac{1}{n}$$

Charge and current

charge = current × time

$$Q = It$$

Resistance, p.d. (voltage) and current

$$\text{resistance} = \frac{\text{p.d.}}{\text{current}}$$

$$R = \frac{V}{I}$$

Resistors in series ...

total resistance $R = R_1 + R_2$

... and in parallel

$$\frac{1}{R} = \frac{1}{R_1} + \frac{1}{R_2}$$

Electrical power

power = p.d. × current = current^2 × resistance

$$P = VI \qquad\qquad = I^2 R$$

Electrical energy

energy transferred = power × time

$$= \text{p.d.} \times \text{current} \times \text{time}$$

$$E = VIt$$

Transformers

$$\frac{\text{output voltage}}{\text{input voltage}} = \frac{\text{output turns}}{\text{input turns}}$$

$$\frac{V_2}{V_1} = \frac{n_2}{n_1}$$

For 100% efficient transformer:

power input = power output

$$\frac{V_1}{I_2} = \frac{V_1}{I_2}$$

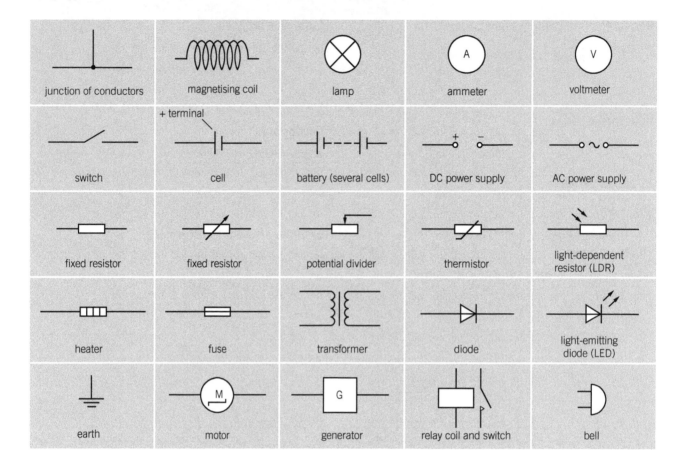

junction of conductors	magnetising coil	lamp	ammeter	voltmeter
switch	+ terminal cell	battery (several cells)	DC power supply	AC power supply
fixed resistor	fixed resistor	potential divider	thermistor	light-dependent resistor (LDR)
heater	fuse	transformer	diode	light-emitting diode (LED)
earth	motor	generator	relay coil and switch	bell

quantity	unit	symbol
mass	kilogram	kg
length	metre	m
time	second	s
area	square metre	m^2
volume	cubic metre	m^3
force	newton	N
weight	newton	N
pressure	pascal	Pa
energy	joule	J
work	joule	J
power	watt	W
frequency	hertz	Hz
p.d., e.m.f. (voltage)	volt	V
current	ampere	A
resistance	ohm	Ω
charge	coulomb	C
capacitance	farad	F
temperature	kelvin	K
	degree Celsius	°C

prefix	meaning	
G (giga)	1 000 000 000	(10^9)
M (mega)	1 000 000	(10^6)
k (kilo)	1000	(10^3)
d (deci)	$\dfrac{1}{10}$	(10^{-1})
c (centi)	$\dfrac{1}{100}$	(10^{-2})
m (milli)	$\dfrac{1}{1000}$	(10^{-3})
µ (micro)	$\dfrac{1}{1\,000\,000}$	(10^{-6})
n (nano)	$\dfrac{1}{1\,000\,000\,000}$	(10^{-9})
p (oica)	$\dfrac{1}{1\,000\,000\,000\,000}$	(10^{-12})

Answers

1 Measurement of physical quantities such as length, volume or force

1. • Clearly named control variable and clear description of how that variable is to be controlled, e.g. roll the balls on the same surface so the friction is the same and the angle is the same, same material for each ball so the friction between the ball and the surface is the same.
   • Appropriate apparatus, e.g. a rule to measure length, vernier callipers to measure the diameter of the ball.
   • A detailed valid plan that will allow the distance to be measured and the volume of the ball to be calculated.
   • Repeat measurements for each variable to allow for reliable results.
   • Taking an average of the repeats to allow for anomalous results, e.g. measure the diameter of the ball in 3 different places and calculate the mean; measure the distance travelled 3 times and calculate the mean.
   • Draw a line graph with distance travelled (the dependent variable) on the vertical axis and volume (the independent variable) on the horizontal axis, with units given.

2. a. i   3.3 cm
      ii. 0.6 cm
      iii. 3.2 cm
   b. The scale is not small enough
      It would not be possible to tell the difference between i and iii
   c. i. It does not sit on the line of best fit/it does not follow the trend of the data. It is an anomalous result.
      ii. 7 ohms
      iii. The line of best fit must go through (0, 0) because if the nail has no length, then no resistance can be measured.
   d. No
      A needle is made of a different material to a nail
      They have different diameters
      Everything apart from the length needs to be controlled to make it a fair test
      It is better to use wire that can be cut to a specific length

3. a. $2 \times 5 \times 5 = 50\,cm^3$
   b. The student will measure the displacement of liquid
      This is equal to the volume of the object

4. a. Add units in table heading
      Use g or kg for mass
      Use mm, cm, or m for length
      Use s or min for time
   b. The student is measuring the horizontal distance which is shorter than the distance travelled along the slope
      The length of the slope (the hypotenuse) should be measured

5. a. 6 N
      64 N
      42 N
   b. There is no human error
      It is more accurate
      It can draw a graph of force against time
      It does not just give a final value

2 Measurement of small distances or short intervals of time

1. a. Advantages: Very accurate
      Good for measuring small distances
      Disadvantage: Hard to read if you don't know how to
   b. The digital scale reduces mistakes when reading a value.

2. a. i. $96 \div 10 = 9.6\,cm$
      ii. Dividing the total distance by the number of waves gives an average value
          This reduces the possibility of anomalous results
          It is more accurate/less chance of error
   b. Place a ruler in the tank and take a photo
      Measure the distance for 10 waves (or similar method)
      Work out the average distance between waves

3. Measure the time for 10 swings
   Work out an average time per swing by dividing the total time by 10
   Small errors in measuring will be minimised

4. a. $1000 - 320 = 680\,ms$
   b. Any 4 from:
      No human error due to the reaction time when starting and stopping the stop watch
      Less chance of error
      Less uncertainty in the measurements
      More accurate
      They can measure very short times with precision
      Reproducible

3 Determining a derived quantity

1. a. Length of the spring (not extension)
   b. Weight = mass × gravitational field strength
   c. $0.2 \times 10 = 2\,N$
   d. i. BC   ii. GH
   e.

Weight (N)	Length of spring (cm)	Extension of spring (cm)
0	9	0
1	13	4
2	15	6
3	17	8
4	19	10
5	21	12
6	23	14

One mark for correct calculation of extensions
   f. Correct scale and labelling of x-axis

Answers

Correct scale and labelling of *y*-axis
At least 5 points plotted correctly
Straight line of best fit, going through origin

g. Directly proportional/direct proportion
The graph is a straight line through the origin

h. The limit of proportionality will be reached
The graph will no longer be a straight line
The graph will start to curve upwards

i. Change in length = 23 − 9 = 14 cm
14 ÷ 9 × 100 = 156%

j. Find the inverse of the gradient of the graph/calculate (change in weight)/extension

k. Lines drawn on graph to show calculation of gradient
When the weight is 6 N,
the extension is 14 cm = 0.14 m

$$k = \frac{F}{x}$$

k = (change in weight) ÷ extension
= 6 ÷ 0.14 = 42.9 N/m

l. Spring could snap and damage eyes

m. To indicate the bottom of the spring

n. This is a direct measurement of the value that has actually changed. The extension is the difference between two measurements of length and is not measured directly.

o. An accurate measurement is close to the true value

2. Hang object of unknown mass from the spring
Measure the length of the spring and calculate the extension
Use the value of the extension and the graph of extension against weight to determine the weight of the object
Use *W* = *mg* to calculate the mass

3. The graphs for the two springs will have different gradients
The stiffer spring will have a lower gradient (because the spring constant is greater)/the less stiff spring will have a higher gradient (because the spring constant is lower)
(Any sketch will only gain marks if clearly labelled)

4. **a.** Applied force = spring constant × extension or *F* = *k* × *x*
b. 5 cm = 0.05 m
Using *F* = *k*/*x*,
3 = *k* 0.05,
so *k* 3/0.05 =60 N/m
x>= 12/60 = 0.2 m = 20 cm
Alternatively, as the extension is directly proportional to the applied force: 12/3 = 4 so the extension will be 4 × 0.05 = 0.2 m

5. **a.** An object's **acceleration** depends on the **force** acting on the object and the **mass** of the object.
b. 0.8 × 5 = 4 N
c. The mass should have been placed on the car (not on the bench)
To keep the mass within the system the same the whole time (control variable)
This will give inaccurate results

d. To reduce friction between the string and the bench

e. The value of the force will be lower
Friction and air resistance act in the opposite direction to the force causing motion
So the resultant force would be lower than the expected value

f. It is difficult to time exactly when the trolley passes the line
Make a video recording of the experiment with a timer and play it back

g. i. 1.5 ÷ 1.25 = 1.2 m/s²
ii. The theoretical values don't take friction into account
The resultant force is smaller than the force pulling on the trolley
Therefore the acceleration is not as great

h. Light gates mean less chance of error when timing results
The original method is simpler to set up
The original method is less expensive
The student's method B can be set up to measure acceleration directly

i. Pull from string forwards horizontally on trolley (arrow longer than air resistance arrow)
Friction/air resistance backwards horizontally
Weight vertically downwards from centre of trolley (arrow same length as reaction force)
(Normal) reaction force vertically upwards from ground at wheels

6. **a.**

Contact force	Non-contact force
friction	gravity
push	air resistance
pull	

b. A scalar quantity has size (magnitude) only
A vector has size and a direction

c. i. Appropriate scale on *x*-axis
Appropriate scale on *y*-axis
All points plotted correctly
Straight line of best fit drawn
ii. Direct proportion

d. i. Both axis labelled with title and units
Straight line of best fit drawn
ii. One calculation shown

10 N

e. $a = \dfrac{\Delta v}{t} = \dfrac{5.1 - 4.5}{3} = 0.2 \, m/s^2$

$F = ma = 1.5 \times 0.2 = 0.3 \, N$

f. i. $a = \dfrac{v^2 - u^2}{2s}$

ii. $a = \dfrac{3.87^2 - 0^2}{2 \times 0.3} = 25.0 \, m/s^2$

iii. $F = ma = 0.200 \times 25.0 = 5.00 \, N$

$5 \div 9.8 = 0.51 \, kg = 510 \, g$

4 The relationship between two variables

1. a. The voltmeter and ammeter are in the wrong places/ the voltmeter should be connected across the component and the ammeter should be in series with it

   b. Close the switch

   c. The ammeter records the current in the circuit and the voltmeter records the potential difference across two points in the circuit.

   d. Any two points 20 cm apart

   e. The ammeter/voltmeter does not read zero when there is no current flowing in the circuit

   f. A straight line must be straight through the origin, from bottom left to top right

   g. Direct proportion

2. a. Test 2 for 60 cm

      15.67 circled

   b. Anomaly discarded: the mean values are:
      4.25; 8.52; 12.79; 16.41; 19.43

   c. The temperature of the wire was not controlled/the temperature increased for each repeat
      Resistance increases with increased temperature, so the results became less repeatable because the values recorded increased with each repeat

   d. Suitable scales on each axis
      All points plotted correctly (±1/2 square)
      Straight line of best fit starting at (0, 0)

   e. The resistance would decrease
      There is more space for the current to flow through

   f. A high current leads to an increase in temperature
      Particles in the wire vibrate faster
      More electrons collide more often with metal ions
      The resistance will increase

5 Measured quantities such as angles of refraction and reflection

1. a. i.

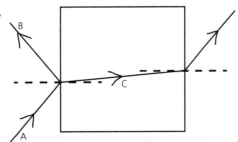

ii. A — Incident ray   B — Reflected ray
    C — Refracted ray

iii. The emergent ray is parallel to the incident ray.

b. Width of ray of light makes the drawing inaccurate
   Measurement error with protractor

c. The angle of refraction would be 90°
   There is no refraction

d. Water waves in a ripple tank

2. a. Set the angle of incidence at the same value for each test
      Easier to see if results are reproducible
      Easier to see the differences between the two materials

   b. The surface may not be perfectly flat

   c. Light bends/the direction changes
      Either towards or away from the normal

   d. Light travel at different speeds in different materials
      When light hits a boundary between two different materials at an angle, one side of the beam/wave hits the new material first
      This side of the beam/wave changes speed first
      So each side of a beam of light/wave is moving different speeds
      So the direction changes/light bends

   e. The difference between the refractive indices of the two materials

   f. Comparison of data from table
      The rays are refracted more in Perspex than in glass
      Light travels more slowly in Perspex

   g. No refraction/total internal reflection occurs

3. Advantages of simulations: no time spent setting up practical equipment; you know the equipment is going to work; students have the chance to work individually and each do the experiment
   Disadvantages of simulations: requires computers; requires internet access
   Advantages of hands-on experiments: students are able to see the results themselves/take measurements themselves; students gain practical experience; potentially cheaper
   Disadvantages for hands-on experiments: time consuming; the equipment might not work
   [1 mark for each opinion and justification (they must match). The other marks can be gained from a balanced answer – students cannot gain all the marks for advantages or disadvantages only]

4. a. Incident and reflected rays drawn on same side of plane mirror
      Normal drawn at 90° to the plane mirror
      Angles measured between each ray and the normal
      Angle of incidence = 65° ± 1°
      Angle of incidence = angle of reflection

   b. i. incident and refracted ray drawn on opposite sides of block

angles measured between ray and normal
angle of incidence = 35° ±1°
angle of refraction = 22° ±1°
normal drawn at 90° to the plane

   ii. $n = \dfrac{\sin i}{\sin r}$; $n = \dfrac{\sin 35°}{\sin 22°} = 1.53$

6 Comparing derived quantities such as density

1. **a.** • regularly shaped solid material
   • irregularly shaped solid material
   • liquid in a regularly shaped container
   • balance
   • ruler (30 cm is long enough)
   • measuring cylinder

   b. **i.** pebble – balance and measuring cylinder/method B
   ii. textbook – balance and ruler/method A
   iii. block of modelling clay – balance and ruler/method A

   c. The volume of the object

   d. To get an accurate value for the volume

   e. Not collecting all the water displaced
   Not fully submerging the object
   Inaccurate reading of the volume of liquid displaced
   not taking reading at bottom of meniscus

   f. **i.** density = mass ÷ volume
   ii. 65 g = 0.065 kg
   50 cm³ = 50 ÷ 1 000 000 = 0.000 05 m³
   Density = 0.065 ÷ 0.000 05 = 1300 kg/m³

   g. **i.** 50 × 50 × 50 = 125 000 cm³
   ii. Mass = volume × density
   4.2 × 125 000
   525 000 g
   525 kg

   h. 1 ml = 1 cm³
   Water has a density of 1 g/cm³
   Honey has a density of 87 ÷ 60 = 1.45 g/cm³
   Honey has a higher density than water/water has a lower density than honey

2. **a.** Use of: Volume of a cylinder = $\pi r^2 h$
   Correct substitution: Volume = π × 2² × 5 = 63 cm³

   b. Fill the displacement can to the level just below the spout
   Position a measuring cylinder under the spout
   Carefully place the cylinder of wood in the can without any water splashing out
   Record the volume of water that flows into the measuring cylinder
   Repeat the process after carving
   Subtract the second measurement from the first

   c. Density of wood = 44 ÷ 63 = 0.70 g/cm³
   Volume of chess piece = 33 ÷ 0.7 = 47 cm³

   d. C
   The resolution of balance will show if the value has been rounded/it shows the measurement to one more decimal place than the given value

3. Mass of liquid = 142.8 − 64.6 = 78.2 g
   Density of liquid = 78.2 ÷ 85 = 0.92 g/cm³
   The liquid is most likely to be olive oil7 Cooling and heating experiments

7 Cooling and heating experiments, including measurement of temperature

1. **a.** Three from:
   mass
   volume
   starting temperature
   surface area

   b. matt-black can
   The final temp is lower so more energy (infrared radiation) has been transferred to the surroundings

   c. silver:
   98° − 62° = 36°
   36 ÷ 300 = 0.12 °C/s
   matt black:
   98° − 49° = 49°
   49 ÷ 300 = 0.16 °C/s

   d. **i.** Axes drawn and labelled correctly
   All points plotted correctly
   Curve of best fit drawn
   ii. Tangent drawn at 150 seconds and gradient calculated
   e.g. 15 × 120 = 0.125 °C

   e. Fill cans with cold/room temperature water
   Record the temperature with a thermometer
   Place the lamp a fixed distance from the cans
   Turn the lamp on and start the timer
   Record the temperature at regular intervals
   The better absorber of radiation will have a faster increase in temperature/higher final temperature

   f. More accurate recording of data
   Continuous monitoring so can take more data points
   Computer can be set up to plot graph as experiments happen
   Experiment can be left unattended

2. **a.** Make sure the infrared detector/thermometer is always the same distance from the surface being tested

   b. The type of surface

   c. y-axis labelled with units, and an appropriate scale
   x-axis labelled all bars correct height

   d. Calculation of difference in amount of infrared radiation:
   shiny silver − matt silver = 35 − 17 = 18 units
   matt black − shiny black = 47 − 39 = 8 units
   shiny black − shiny silver = 39 − 17 = 22 units

matt black − matt silver = 47 − 35 = 12 units
There is a bigger difference between the amount of radiation emitted by surfaces of different colours than between surfaces with different roughness
The data supports the hypothesis
Matt black emits more than shiny silver
Matt surfaces emit more than shiny
Black emits more than silver

  e. Matt black is the best absorber
Matt surface irregular/black reflects less infrared
Shiny silver surface is the worst absorber
Shiny surface reflects infrared

3. a. Transferred to surroundings/dissipated to surroundings
   b. i. To stop energy being transferred to surroundings by evaporation/convection
      ii. To measure equal amounts of water into each container
      iii. To measure the temperature change in each container
   c. More accurate recording of data
Continuous monitoring so can take more data points
Computer can be set up to plot graph as experiments happen
The experiment can be left unattended
   d. Measuring cylinder (pipette or burette are also valid answers)
   e. Line graph − shows continuous data
Bar chart − shows discrete data
   f. i. Energy transferred = 0.8 × 4.2 × (84 − 61)
         = 77.28 J
      ii. Percentage change = $\frac{(84-61)}{(84)} \times 100\% = 27.4\%$ (decrease)
   g. 0.9 × 60 = 54 °C
65 − 54 = 11 °C
Water will not cool below room temperature so the temperature after 1 hour will be 25 °C

4. a. B would have greater decrease in temperature
The air in unpopped bubble wrap is a good thermal insulator
Popping the bubbles means less insulation so a faster transfer of energy to the surroundings

5. a. Appropriate scale and label on x-axis
Appropriate scale and labelling on y-axis
9 points plotted correctly
Curved line of best fit drawn
   b. Construction lines shown
Value in the range of 1.1 to 1.5
Unit °C/minute

6. a. Aimee is correct/cotton wool is the best insulator
It had the smallest temperature change of 21 °C whereas bubble wrap had a temperature change of 30 °C
   b. Plot the temperature change

Use the same starting temperature for the water in each container

7. a. An ammeter should be connected in series.
A voltmeter should be connected in parallel.
   b. The group that used the insulation would have more accurate results
Insulation stops energy loss to the surroundings
The experiment with no insulation will lose energy to heat the air surrounding the block
The values for energy transferred/work done will be inaccurate leading to inaccurate graphs
The value calculated from the gradient will be inaccurate.
   c. Measure the time for a larger temperature increase
To reduce the percentage error in the measurement
   d. To give an even temperature/to make good thermal contact/to allow the thermometer to get an accurate reading
   e. Aluminium; it has the highest specific heat capacity, so it needs more energy to change the temperature
   f. i. It allows continuous monitoring
It is guaranteed to record the highest temperature
      ii. It is more expensive than a thermometer
   g. i. Appropriate scale on x-axis
Appropriate scale on y-axis
At least 8 of the points plotted correctly
Correct line of best fit (curved then straight)
Construction lines when working out gradient
Identification of steel as the metal with a specific heat capacity of 452 J/Kg °C
      ii. Not all of the data is given to the same number of decimal places
It is important to keep the resolution of data the number of decimal places the same
   h. It takes time for the block to warm up, so there won't be a linear transfer of energy to the water.

8. P = IV = 1.2 × 12 = 14.4 W
E = P × t = 14.4 × 240 = 3456 J
Mass = energy/(specific heat capacity × temperature change)
       = 3456 ÷ (385 × 8) = 1.1 kg
Correct units must be given

8 Timing motion or oscillations

1. a. Take an image with a camera/video/phone
Use a metre rule in image as scale bar
Measure the wavelength and calculate value from scale bar
   b. The lamp casts shadows of the waves on the white screen, which makes it easier to see/count the waves
   c. 22 ÷ 5.0 = 4.4 Hz
   d. i. Use a metre rule
Create stationary waves (or named method, e.g. use strobe lighting, take an image)
      ii. Timer

Count the number of waves going past a set point for a measured period of time

e. Student B will get the most accurate data
The effect of errors in measuring will be lower than for student A, as any error will be divided by 10

f. The waves will be regular/have constant frequency
The frequency can easily be changed
It is possible to produce high frequency waves

g. Wave speed = frequency × wavelength

h. Count the waves passing a fixed point on the screen in a fixed time
Use a long time interval to improve accuracy/reduce error
Divide the number of waves by the number of seconds to calculate the frequency
Measure the distance between as many waves as possible
Divide the distance by the number of waves to calculate the wavelength
Use $v = f\lambda$ to calculate the wave speed

i. Frequency = 17 ÷ 11 = 1.5454 Hz
Wavelength = 0.5 ÷ 10 = 0.05 m
Wave speed = frequency × wavelength
$= 1.5455 \times 0.05 = 0.077$ m/s

2. a. Measure half a wavelength
Multiply number by 2

b. Change the frequency
Change the length of the string
Change the mass placed on the end of the string

c. Wavelength = wave speed ÷ frequency
$= 5100 \div 5600 = 0.91$ m = 91 cm

9 Electrical circuits

1. a. $9\,\Omega$

b. In a series circuit, the total resistance is the sum of the resistances of each resistor
Resistors in parallel have the same potential difference across each of them
The total resistance in a parallel circuit is the sum of the reciprocals $\left(\frac{1}{R}\right)$ of the individual resistances

c. $I = \frac{Q}{t}$
3 minutes = 180 seconds
$I = \frac{9}{180} = 0.05$ A
$V = \frac{E}{Q} = \frac{45}{9} = 5$ V
$R = \frac{V}{I} = \frac{5}{0.05} = 100\ \Omega$

2. a. Components may get hot after being on for a while, so you should not touch them.
Do not allow the current to go above 1.0 A, as this could cause overheating.
Always switch off the power supply or disconnect the batteries before building or changing your circuit, to prevent electrocution

b.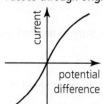

bulb

battery

thermistor

diode

c. Axes labelled correctly
Correct curved line drawn
Passes through origin

d. The graph is initially a straight line through the origin
The filament gets hot
The resistance increases as the temperature increases
The current is no longer proportional to the potential difference so gradient flattens
gradient = 1/resistance, so the gradient decreases as the temperature increases and the resistance increases
It is harder for electrons to pass through a wire when it is hotter because the lattice atoms are vibrating more and obstructing the flow

e. i. Component 1: points plotted correctly
Correct line of best fit
Component 2: points plotted correctly
Correct line of best fit

ii. Component 1 = resistor (fixed or ohmic)
Component 2 = diode

iii. For a diode:
no current flows on the negative side of the graph as the resistance in very high
the resistance is very high at low voltage
as the voltage increases, the resistance falls quickly
in a diode, current can only flow in one direction, whereas in a fixed resistor it can flow in both directions
For a resistor:
resistance is constant
therefore current and voltage are proportional
the graph of current against voltage is a straight line through the origin

iv. 0.2 A

v. Construction of large gradient triangle
Resistance = change in potential difference/change in current
$= 3 \div 0.15 = 20\,\Omega$

f. To be able to measure the effect of reversing

the current/if the component is a diode, no current will flow; if it is a resistor it will

g. To measure very small currents with a high resolution

2. a. $7.4 \div 14.8 = 0.5$

$0.5 \times 9.2 = 4.6V$

b. When no current is flowing there cannot be any potential difference

c. $I = V \div R$

$= \frac{2}{5} = 0.4A$

10 Optics experiments

1. a. u = distance between the centre of the lens and the lamp

v = distance between the centre of the lens and the screen

b. Next to the lamp

c. Measure the distance from the illuminated object to the screen (D)

Change the distance from the illuminated object to the screen (D)

Alter the position of the lens to get a clear image

Record u and v

Draw a graph of uv against D

The gradient is the focal length

d. It is not possible to measure the exact distance to the centre of the lens

Too much ambient light in the room

2. a. Data logger/ light probe

b. Intensity of light

Distance of light source from material

Thickness of material

Colour of light

c. A ray box or a laser pointer

Title:

Stage 1: Note observations

Stage 2: Formulate a question

Stage 3: Create a hypothesis

Stage 4: Conduct experiments

Stage 5: Record results

Stage 6: Report results

Name:

Date:

Title:

Stage 1: Note observations	**Stage 2: Formulate a question**
Stage 3: Create a hypothesis	**Stage 4: Conduct experiments**
Stage 5: Record results	**Stage 6: Report results**

Name:	Date:

Title:

Stage 1: Note observations	**Stage 2: Formulate a question**
Stage 3: Create a hypothesis	**Stage 4: Conduct experiments**
Stage 5: Record results	**Stage 6: Report results**

Name:

Date:

Title:

Stage 1: Note observations	**Stage 2: Formulate a question**
Stage 3: Create a hypothesis	**Stage 4: Conduct experiments**
Stage 5: Record results	**Stage 6: Report results**